LEADERSHIP

LEADERSHIP

BRIAN TRACY

AMACOM AMERICAN MANAGEMENT ASSOCIATION
New York • Atlanta • Brussels • Chicago • Mexico City
San Francisco • Shanghai • Tokyo • Toronto • Washington, D.C.

Bulk discounts available. For details visit:
www.amacombooks.org/go/specialsales
Or contact special sales:
Phone: 800-250-5308 / E-mail: specialsls@amanet.org
View all the AMACOM titles at: www.amacombooks.org

Library of Congress Cataloging-in-Publication Data

Tracy, Brian.
Leadership / Brian Tracy.
    p. cm.
Includes index.
ISBN 978-0-8144-3341-6 — ISBN 0-8144-3341-3 1. Leadership. I. Title.
HD57.7.T725 2014
658.4'092—dc23

                                                                2013042969

About AMA

American Management Association (www.amanet.org) is a world leader in talent development, advancing the skills of individuals to drive business success. Our mission is to support the goals of individuals and organizations through a complete range of products and services, including classroom and virtual seminars, webcasts, webinars, podcasts, conferences, corporate and government solutions, business books, and research. AMA's approach to improving performance combines experiential learning—learning through doing—with opportunities for ongoing professional growth at every step of one's career journey.

Printing number
10 9 8 7 6 5 4

CONTENTS

Introduction

OLIVER WENDELL HOLMES, the great Supreme Court Justice, once said that there are three types of people. There are people who make things happen, there are people who watch what's happening, and there are people who haven't the slightest idea what's happening.

In this book, we're going to talk about leadership in action and about the people who make things happen.

There is a need for leadership in our society. There is a need for leadership in our homes, in our business organizations, in our private and public associations, and in our government. We need leadership more than ever before. And especially, we need leadership to take us into the future. We need people who have vision and courage, people with the ability to chart new seas and break new ground.

We need two types of leaders. The first type is the most important or foundational: the *transactional* leader. The transactional leader is the person who gets things done with and through others.

The second type of leader that we need is the *transformational* leader. This is the leader who is the path maker. This is the leader who is the visionary. This is the leader who motivates, uplifts, inspires, and empowers people to perform at levels far beyond anything they've ever done before.

The reason we need leadership so badly in our institutions, and especially in our businesses, is because the people working in today's businesses and institutions are far more difficult and demanding, far more analytical, and more selfish than they have ever been before.

It's no longer enough just to give someone a job and to tell the person what to do. People want to participate. They want to discuss their jobs. They want regular feedback on their performance. They want to know, "What's in it for me?" Today, more and more, when individuals go out to look for a job, they adopt the attitude, "Why should I work for you?"

One of the major reasons people go to work for any organization is because of the leadership. There are two great definitions of leadership that I like, especially with regard to business organizations. The first is this:

Leadership is the ability to elicit extraordinary performance from ordinary people.

Another definition is:

Leadership is the ability to get followers.

Today, leadership that comes from position or from money or authority (what's called ascribed leadership) is short-lived. The only kind of leadership that is lasting is where people *decide* that they are going to follow the direction, the guidance, and the vision of someone else. In other words, it is the voluntary form of following that marks our best leaders today.

ONE

Leaders Are Made, Not Born

I'VE BEEN STUDYING leadership for many years. I started when I was a teenager, and the first leader that I studied at length was Hannibal of Carthage. I read book after book about the Punic Wars, the capabilities of Hannibal's elephants crossing the Alps, and the battles against the Romans. He was able to take a very small force, mold it into a powerful fighting force, take it thousands of miles, and almost defeat the greatest empire of his time.

After that, I studied Scipio, the general who defeated Hannibal. I studied the life of Napoleon and Wellington at great length as well, to understand the differences between the two men. I've also studied Washington and Lincoln and Generals George Patton, Dwight Eisenhower, and Omar Bradley, who were some of the great leaders of their time.

What I have found is that leaders are made, not born. Nobody comes into the world a natural leader. Even Alexander the Great studied (from the age of eight) to become a leader.

Study the Greats

The study of great leaders of the past and present is one of the fastest and surest ways to develop leadership qualities. The more you study what constitutes effective leadership, the more likely you will be to internalize the same values and behaviors. These values and behaviors will then be externalized in your actions and in your results.

Abraham Lincoln wrote, "That some have succeeded is proof that others can as well." Bertrand Russell, the great philosopher, agreed, writing: "The very best proof that something can be done is the fact that others have already done it."

Think about the men and women you know of who are leaders that you admire, and then begin to think about how you could emulate their behaviors. Think about how you could be more like them. And lo and behold, over a reasonable period of time, you actually begin to absorb their qualities and become a leader yourself.

The Story of Alexander

The story of Alexander the Great is very instructive for anyone who aspires to a high leadership position. By the age of fifteen, Alexander was convinced that it was his destiny to conquer the known world. He had a vision of uniting all mankind in a common brotherhood. With Aristotle as his teacher, he studied and prepared himself for many years. He learned the military arts from his father and his father's best generals. He saw himself as a great king and had an unshakable belief in his ability to achieve any goal he ever set for himself.

Alexander was brilliant at both administration and execution. He showed great judgment in delegating and appointed the right officers in the right positions at the right time. He was able to plan, organize, think through, and execute brilliantly.

At the Battle of Arbela, he led his 50,000 men in a full frontal assault on the one-million-strong Persian army and routed them. He never entertained the possibility of defeat. He had complete trust in himself, in his men, and in their ability to overcome any difficulty, no matter how great the odds against them.

Alexander, like all great leaders, had the ability to organize his men and inspire them to exceed anything they had ever done before. He had the ability to concentrate on his strengths and to focus on the critical areas that were essential for victory. His life and history are an example of the blending together of all the great leadership qualities that have been identified in every study on the subject.

See Yourself as a Leader

In the introduction, I expressed the idea that there is a spectrum where, at the very bottom, we find people who haven't

the slightest idea what's going on (and couldn't care less), while at the very top there are the one or two percent of people in our society who really are the spark plugs in the engines of change. Every one of us is on that spectrum somewhere, moving up or down, depending on the things that we are doing and saying on a daily basis.

If you want to be a leader or a better leader, remember that it's all up to you. It's in your hands, or, even more important, in your mind. You are what you think you are. Your self-image determines your performance. You can become a much more effective leader by changing your self-concept—the way you think about yourself as a leader.

It all begins with the Law of Cause and Effect. It is the basic law of the universe; all other laws in the fields of mathematics or any of the sciences are subsets of this law, which says that for every effect there is cause. Nothing just happens. The implication of this law is powerful. It means that the success of every person has a cause or causes. So, if you want to be as successful as someone else, if you want to emulate successful people and how they acted and what they accomplished, then find out what they did and do the same! Do the same things successful people do, over and over again, and eventually you will get the same results.

A related law is the Law of Belief. It states that if you believe in something with conviction, what you believe in will become your reality. Or to put it another way, you are what you believe you are. Philosopher William James said, "Belief creates the actual fact."

The purpose of this book is to enable you to become a leader—and if you are already a leader, to enable you to become a more effective leader. I'll do that by describing to you some of the qualities, attributes, and behaviors of the most effective leaders in our society so that you can emulate those qualities and make them your reality.

TWO

A Sense of Mission

LEADERS HAVE a vision and a sense of mission that lifts up and inspires men and women to help achieve that mission. In fact, there is in every one of us a desire to commit to something bigger than ourselves; leaders have the ability to tap into that root of motivation, drive, and enthusiasm that allows us to commit ourselves to achieving that vision.

As a leader, then, you have to have a goal that excites and inspires. And the only goals that excite and inspire are goals that are qualitative. Nobody gets excited or inspired about raising the share price or making more money or getting a raise. But we do get inspired and excited about bringing a product or service to people who need it, and about being the best, and about winning great success in a competitive field.

Strive to Be the Best

As a leader, the most important vision you can have for yourself is to be the best. And that same vision must apply to your business or your organization. You will accept nothing less for yourself or your company than to be the best at what you do. In business, that means asking:

> *What quality about your product or service is most relevant or important to your customers?*

Once you've identified that quality, focus all the energies and creativity of your employees and managers on achieving superior performance in that area.

We need to be the best. You won't feel great or as good as you could feel, or capable of extraordinary performance, unless you are aligned with the best people in your field and doing the very best job that people are capable of.

Instill Meaning and Purpose

Being dedicated to a mission gives work meaning and purpose. As human beings, we need meaning and purpose as much as we need food and water and air. We need a sense of significance. And leaders are those people who make us feel significant. They make us feel important and remind us that what we are doing has value far beyond just the day-to-day work. They make us feel that we are an integral part of the mission team.

There are four ways to make people feel important, and they each start with the letter *A*. First is *appreciation*. Take every opportunity to thank people for the quality of their work and their role in making the company a success. Every time you thank individuals, they are going to feel more valuable and will be more motivated to justify your faith in them.

The second way to make people feel more important and valuable is by showing *approval*. Praise people at every opportunity, for any accomplishment, large or small. Praise them also for their suggestions and insight—for their thinking. People will take praise emotionally. Their self-esteem and self-worth rises. But it's important to praise immediately and specifically, so that people know that it is genuine.

The third way you can build a sense of importance and value in a person is through *admiration*. Continually compliment people, whether it's on their traits, such as persistence, on their possessions, such as clothes, or on their accomplishments.

Perhaps the most important way for people to feel important and valued is through *attention*. People aren't going to be dedicated to the goals of the organization if they are continuously ignored. They are not going to feel like key players in the mission if they just receive commands without having any opportunity for input or feedback. Attention means listening to people, without interrupting. You don't necessarily have to take their suggestions or agree to what they are saying. But give them a chance to say it.

A Common Cause

A good goal or a good mission gives a clear sense of direction not only to the organization, but to every person in the organization.

A good goal unifies everyone in a common cause. For example, IBM is one of the great industrial leaders of business history. One of its goals is to give the very best customer service of any company in the entire world. One of its missions is to be known as the company that cares for its customers. This mission, which involves a qualitative not a quantitative goal, excites and inspires people throughout the company because they think about it and talk about it all the time. They believe they're the best and that nobody takes care of customers like they do at IBM. Everyone in the company knows that his job, one way or another, is related to taking care of customers, and this knowledge unifies everybody in a common cause.

The mission of a company will often be encapsulated in a mission statement. A mission statement is a clear statement of why the company exists in the first place and what its overarching goal or purpose is. Mission statements usually involve the customer in some way—for example, how your product or service is going to help make the customer's life better. YouTube founder Chad Hurley wanted people to be able to send homemade videos over the Internet. Charles Schwab's mission was to be the "most useful and ethical financial services company." Google founders Larry Page and Sergey Brin wanted to make navigating the Internet easier.

Why does your company exist? What is its cause?

The Core Purpose of Every Business

For a business leader, there is one core purpose above all, and that is to acquire and serve a customer. Leaders make the customer of the organization the central focus. Take the example of Nordstrom, whose leaders think incessantly and continuously about their customers. IBM thinks and talks about only its customers. More and more companies are becoming obsessed with the customer. You see, once everybody agrees on who the customer is and agrees that the purpose of the company is to satisfy that customer the very best way possible, then it's easy to get everybody pulling together.

As a matter of fact, I believe that you can tell how well led an organization is by applying a very simple test. When you're in that organization, look at and listen to how people refer to the customer. In a good organization, the customers are always referred to with respect. They are always referred to with pride, as though they are really important. When a customer calls, it is an important occasion. And when a customer has a problem and is helped, it is a cause for celebration. When a customer calls and is happy or satisfied with a product or service, everybody takes on a tremendous feeling of pride and accomplishment.

In your organization, how do people talk about the customer?

Let's say you run a department that services another department within the organization. That other department is your customer. Whoever has to use what you produce in your area of responsibility is your customer. And leaders have to be very much focused on satisfying that customer.

If you are going to be a business leader or a leader of a department or any organization, you have to sit down and think through what the mission or the overarching purpose or goal is going to be for that business or department. It is the determination of a mission to be the best, that does something to help others, that is the starting point of your ascension and rise to the top of leadership.

Action Orientation

When you look at the life of Napoleon or Alexander the Great, or Florence Nightingale or Mother Teresa, you'll find that they were incredibly active men and women all the time. They were not contemplative and waiting for things to happen. They were people who had an idea, a concept, and a mission and then launched.

Leaders are innovative and entrepreneurial. Entrepreneurial comes from a French word meaning "to undertake or to do." Innovative means trying new things and getting on with them. Leaders don't analyze things to death.

This is the motto of the business leader of today: Do it. Fix it. Try it. It comes from the Tom Peters book *In Search of Excellence,* where he says that top companies are those that make more tries, drill more holes, and get on with things.

They don't hesitate and spend months and years on analysis; they get out and do something. As they say, "Don't just do something; move forward."

How Action Saved $2 Million

Leaders are personally action-oriented. They are constantly moving their companies forward, but they are also themselves always active. Don't do something tomorrow that could be done today.

Procrastination is the opposite of action. Leaders don't procrastinate, otherwise they wouldn't be leaders. This is a lesson I learned early in my career. When I was working for a large company, my boss asked me to fly to Reno to begin development work on a $2 million property that the company was purchasing. He said I could go within the next couple of weeks. I wasn't a leader in the company at that time, but since I have never procrastinated, I decided to go the next morning. As soon as I arrived in Nevada and started meeting with people, including the engineer in charge of the development work on the property, I sensed that there was something wrong with the property. By the end of the day, just a few hours before the deal was supposed to close, I realized what was wrong: The property had no water source and was undevelopable. By moving to action immediately, I saved my company from spending $2 million on a worthless piece of land. Needless to say, my boss was happy—and within a year, I was running three divisions and had a staff of forty-two people.

Be Forward Thinking

Leaders are forward thinking. Most leaders live in the future. They are continually focusing their thoughts on the future— what will be and how to create it. Most nonleaders focus on the present and the past. To be forward thinking means establishing a set of goals and focusing every day on moving toward those goals.

Leaders follow these seven steps for achieving goals:

1. *Identify your major goals.* Decide exactly what you want to achieve, whether it's for your business or your life. Clarity is essential.

2. *Write it down.* Be specific and detailed. Make it measurable. As an example, your goal might be to double your sales in the next two years. So, write it down. If your goal is not in writing, it's nothing more than a vague fantasy.

3. *Set a deadline for the achievement of the goal.* If it's a big goal, then break it down into pieces and set deadlines for each of those pieces. We are energized by time-specific goals. Give yourself deadlines.

4. *Make a list of everything that you have to do to achieve each major goal.* Be comprehensive. As you think of more things, add them to the list until it is complete.

5. *Create an action plan.* This is where you take the list and turn it into specific steps. There are two things to think about: priority and sequence. What items on the list are most important? What must be done first? When setting priorities, remember the 80/20 rule: 20 percent of the things you do will account for 80 percent of your results. You don't want to spend your time on unimportant things. You don't want your people spending time on unimportant things. Identify what's really going to help you and your organization to achieve your goals. As for sequence, you have to identify exactly what needs to be done before something else can be done. Any plan is going to have activities that are dependent on certain other activities being done. Also, identify the limitations, constraints, or obstacles that stand in your way. Priority is again important. What are the most important obstacles? What are the things you will absolutely need to overcome before you can achieve your goal?

6. *Take action.* Now that you have a plan, and you know the hurdles on the path before you, you must act—immediately. There can be no more delays. Many people fail because they don't take action on their goals and plans. Leaders don't make that mistake.

7. *Do something every day.* When you get up in the morning, plan your day and then do something, anything, that moves you toward achieving your goals.

Peter Drucker wrote, "The responsibility of the leader is to think about the future; no one else can." Strategic planner Michael Kami says, "Those who do not think about the future cannot have one." Author and management expert Alec Mackenzie says, "The best way to predict the future is to create it." Leaders create the future by setting goals and moving forward, step-by-step, every day, toward those goals.

FOUR

The Quality of Courage

COURAGE IS ONE of the most important qualities of leadership. It is courage that causes the leader to launch, and it is also what causes people to rally around the banner of the leader. Courage, wonderfully enough, can be developed. Courage is not something you are born with, but it is something you can learn.

Courage is something that is a habit. You can develop the habit of courage by practicing it. Whenever you have a tendency to hesitate or back off from a challenge, force yourself to go forward. Always be moving toward the things you fear. You develop the habit of cowardliness by moving from or avoiding the things or people you fear. You must go the other way. Every day, you must make it a habit to confront the things you fear, to face the people or situations you fear.

Each time you face a fear and conquer it, your courage grows. Eventually, just by continually doing the things you fear, you will no longer fear anything.

One of the keys to courage is boldness. One of my favorite lines is, "Act boldly and unseen forces will come to your aid." I have worked with many men and women who've had great success in business and who had limited talents and abilities and resources, yet they had the capacity to launch themselves whenever they got an opportunity.

Somehow, when you launch yourself continually, things seem to work for you. Forces and people and circumstances conspire together to help you accomplish things in ways that you cannot now dream of. Practice boldness. Practice audacity.

A second key to courage is the willingness to initiate action. Leaders don't wait for someone else to do something. You cannot imagine a successful general who waits for the enemy to determine when an attack should take place. Leaders are attack-oriented.

One of the generals I studied was Frederick the Great of Prussia. (He was one of only a few people to be known as "the Great" in his lifetime.) Whenever he met the enemy, no matter how big the forces, he attacked. If you were an enemy force facing Frederick of Prussia, when he came across you, he would attack. If he had 10,000 men and you had 70,000, he would attack you. His motto: *de l'audace, de l'audace, et toujours de l'audace*—audacity, audacity, always audacity.

Now, of course, he lost a lot of battles, but he won the critical ones and became one of the foremost rulers of his day. Eventually other leaders knew that if they crossed Frederick of Prussia, he would always attack with all his forces to defeat them.

Stay the Course

Another mark of courage is the ability to stay the course. This is often called courageous patience. It's what Margaret Thatcher as prime minister of Britain was famous for. No matter how tough it gets, no matter how much tension or stress you face, stay the course and hang in there. Sometimes, if you stay the course long enough and hard enough, the sun will break through the clouds and things will happen for you.

When Germany seemed poised to defeat England and win World War II, Winston Churchill made his most famous speech in which he said, "We will never surrender!" He proclaimed these defiant words even when others were urging him to make peace with Hitler. Privately, he explained why he refused to give in. "I study history," he said. "And history tells you that, if you hold on long enough, something always happens." He was right. Less than a month after this private conversation, the Japanese had bombed Pearl Harbor, Hitler had declared war on the United States, and the greatest industrial power on the planet had now joined forces with Churchill's England.

Dare to Go Forward

Remember that the future belongs to the risk takers. There is no greatness in life among those who avoid taking risks.

Now, that doesn't mean that you have to risk life, limb, and everything you own. It just means that you take calculated risks in the direction of moving forward. Consider the worst possible outcome and do everything possible to minimize unnecessary risks, but then dare to go forward. Perhaps no other quality distinguishes leaders from nonleaders than the willingness and the daring to push forward.

FIVE

The Leader as Strategist

LEADERS ARE GOOD strategists and planners. Again, what I've found in working with successful men and women in business is that they're very, very good planners. They have taken the time to learn or been taught how to do strategic thinking.

Strategic thinking means taking the long view. It means engaging in what is called "big-picture thinking." Leaders look at everything they are doing and at all the different things that can have an impact on them. They look upon themselves as part of a bigger world. They think in terms of "If I do this, what is likely to happen? How will my competition respond; how will friends and enemies respond; what will the market do?"

What May Happen?

Leaders are experts at what I call *extrapolatory thinking*. They can accurately predict what is going to happen in the future based on what is happening today. They look at the current trends of what customers are buying today to decide what kinds of products and services those customers will be buying or expecting in the future.

Leaders also anticipate crises. They don't wait till something happens; they are always asking, "What could go wrong? What could possibly happen that could threaten my business?"

Similar to extrapolatory thinking is *teleological thinking*, which means projecting forward and looking at the different possible outcomes and results before acting. It was said that Napoleon won most of his battles in his tent. He would look at the plan of battle and his maps and consider all the different things that could go wrong and think through what he would do in response to each of those things. In the heat of the battle, when things went against him, he had already thought out completely what to do and was able to give answers instantly.

Good strategic thinkers always have an advantage over people who don't take the time to do the thinking in advance.

Building a Strategic Plan

Leaders must have a strategic plan for their organizations. There are six key questions you must answer to develop an effective plan.

1. *Where are you now?* Any strategic plan begins with a complete assessment of the company's situation. If you don't know your current situation, you won't know what steps your company needs to take to achieve its strategic goals. Be specific. For each business unit or product area, determine your sales, profitability, assets, trends, and competitive position.

2. *How did you get where you are today?* Honesty is the key here. What decisions have led to your current situation? What activities are you doing that are important to your current success? What activities are unnecessary to acquire and keep profitable customers? What activities could be outsourced but are still in-house?

3. *Where do you want to go from here?* Once you've determined where you are today and why (steps 1 and 2), you now must identify where you want to go. Be detailed. Identify, for example, the products you are selling, the customer base you are selling to, and the financial results you'll be achieving in the ideal world five years from now.

4. *How do you get from where you are today to where you want to go?* Make a list of everything that you would have to do to achieve the ideal future you just described. Every time you think of a new task, add it to the list.

5. *What obstacles will you have to overcome to achieve your strategic goals?* There are constraints and limiting factors that are preventing you from being the ideal company described in your strategic plan. What are those constraints and factors, and what are you going to do about them?

6. *What additional knowledge or resources will you need to achieve your strategic objectives?* There are always new core competencies that a company needs to acquire or develop to stay relevant to customers and ahead of its competitors. For example, many companies now have social media experts on their staffs.

The Scenario Planning Tool

One of the best tools for leaders to use for making a strategic plan is scenario planning. The process involves developing three or four detailed scenarios that describe what your company and the business environment might look like five, ten, or twenty years down the road. Each scenario must be detailed in every way, explaining what products you are selling, who your customers are, who your competitors are and what they are doing differently, what outside or environmental influences, such as regulatory bodies, are impacting your business and how. Once you have the future scenario, you work backward to today and figure out what you must do—starting now!—to prepare for the scenarios. If a realistic scenario shows a competitor underselling your product, what can you do now to prevent this situation?

Concentrating Your Forces

One important aspect of good strategy is concentrating your forces by looking at the strengths of yourself, your people, and your organization and focusing them where they can make a major difference. You also want to focus them on the weakest areas of your opposition or competition in the marketplace.

There's no point in going head-to-head with your competition in areas where both of you are strong. But there are always opportunities in the marketplace for a company to take its unique qualities, differentiate its product or service, and go after a specific market segment where its competitors are weak and where it can develop superiority. Though you need to concentrate your forces, also be alert to where you are vulnerable to your competition and give thought to what we call the WPO—the worst possible outcome. What's the worst possible thing that could happen in terms of setbacks? What's the worst possible thing that could happen in terms of markets, interest rates, staff, competitive response, and so on? Think through all of those scenarios so that if the market does throw a ringer at you, you are prepared with a plan.

Strategic planners and leaders have the ability to react quickly because they have thought through what is going on. They are not swamped or carried away by events. They have the ability to see what's happening, take in the situation, and make decisions to redeploy assets and people or to back off in some areas and move forward in others. In many cases, your ability to react quickly to an adverse circumstance is a mark of leadership.

SIX

The Ability to Inspire and Motivate

THE AVERAGE PERSON in our society works at less than 50 percent of capacity, and sometimes at only 40 percent capacity. Leaders draw out of people that 30 percent, 40 percent, or 50 percent of additional capacity and get them to contribute far beyond their previous performance.

Motivation Factors

The first step is to understand what motivates people, what is going to get them to do that extra 30 percent or 50 percent. We have identified six motivation factors that are key to turning average performers into exceptional performers.

The first motivation factor is to give people challenging and interesting work. When employees aren't engaged, non-leaders will look to blame the employees. But are those employees only given mundane tasks that are not interesting in any way? Leaders understand that to motivate people you have to give them a reason to be motivated. Give them work that will stretch them and move them out of their comfort zones and help them grow.

The second factor that motivates people is open communication. Leaders don't just tell employees what to do without any explanation of why they are doing it. Employees will be inspired and motivated if they understand how their tasks fit into the overall picture.

The third factor is responsibility and accountability. If employees are held responsible for the tasks, they are much more likely to be engaged in the task. It also builds up their confidence and self-esteem. Leaders know how to support their employees while at the same time stepping back and giving them full responsibility.

The fourth factor is personal growth and promotion. If employees feel that they are advancing in the skills or learning something new and important, then they will be much more motivated to work as best as they can.

As for the fifth and sixth motivating or inspiring factors, they are the ones that most people think of first! I'm talking about money and working conditions. Money and working conditions will motivate people. But contrary to popular wisdom, they are not the most important motivators.

The Three Emotional Needs

Employees have three types of emotional needs that, if satisfied, will keep them motivated and inspired.

The first is the need for *dependence*, to feel a part of something bigger than ourselves, and it is an important element in an umbrella organization that is doing something important. Continually emphasize to employees that their work is valuable to the goals of the company.

The second type of emotional need is the need for *independence*. In this case, people want to be recognized for their own personal qualities and accomplishments, for what they are achieving as individuals. Make sure that you take every opportunity to make employees feel great about themselves personally.

The third type of emotional need is the need for *interdependence*. This is the need to feel that you are a part of a team, working effectively and cooperatively on the same goals. The best leaders will be constantly seeking ways to keep the working relationships among employees harmonious and productive.

Leaders who can satisfy all three of these emotional needs will have employees who are happy and motivated to work hard and contribute to the success of the company.

The Art of Delegation

Delegation is an important way to inspire and motivate people because it gives them ownership in the tasks and the goals of the department or the company. Here are some of the essentials you need to know about delegating.

First, pick the right person. Delegating a task to the wrong person, for whatever reason, is sure to lead to failure.

Instead of motivating someone, you've done the opposite. Picking the right person is the linchpin of delegation.

Second, match the requirements of the job to the abilities of the person. Does the person have the skills and experience required to get the job done?

Third, delegate effectively to the right person. Look to delegate any tasks that can be done by other people so that you can concentrate your time on the high-value tasks.

Fourth, delegate smaller tasks to newer staff members. This will give them a chance to build up their confidence and grow in their ability to complete larger tasks.

Fifth, delegate the entire job. People are motivated when they have complete responsibility for the job, not when they are given bits and pieces to do.

Sixth, delegate clear outcomes. Explain clearly what needs to be done, and set up metrics to measure the outcome. If you can't measure it, you can't manage it.

Finally, delegate with participation and discussion. Participation is always more motivating than simply being handed a task or responsibility. Invite people to ask questions and make suggestions. It will ensure that they take complete ownership of the task.

When you delegate an assignment, have the employee repeat it back to you. It is absolutely imperative that the employee understands the assignment. Don't delegate an assignment to an employee who is not taking notes. There's a 50 percent chance that the employee is going to misunderstand your instructions, so now is the time to catch the error. If necessary, give the person a piece of paper or writing pad for taking notes.

Be What You Want Them to Be

There are several other ways that leaders inspire and motivate people. One way is to arouse enthusiasm. Leaders recognize that it's up to them to turn their people into enthusiastic participants. When Frances Hesselbein took over as head of the Girl Scouts, the organization was floundering. But Hesselbein knew that the volunteers involved in the organization were looking for a reason to be motivated and inspired. "It's not about creating enthusiasm; it's about releasing it—tapping the incredible energy that people have in their hearts and minds to serve others," Hesselbein says. Hesselbein found a way to tap into that energy, and her complete turnaround of the Girl Scouts earned her the Presidential Medal of Freedom.

Leaders often arouse enthusiasm by being enthusiastic themselves. There is a one-to-one relationship between how excited and enthusiastic you are about what you're doing and how excited and enthusiastic you can make other people. If you are tremendously enthusiastic, then your employees will be enthusiastic as well, although to a lesser degree.

Another way to inspire and motivate others is through your commitment. Leaders are committed 100 percent. One of the characteristics of leaders is that they are all in—100 percent. They are not in for a little bit; they have a sense of total commitment to their work. The level of commitment that you have is going to help determine the commitment of others around you.

By the way, your level of commitment is going to determine the attention that you get from your superiors because highly committed people are always considered more valuable to an organization and preferred for promotions. People who run their own businesses will also find that their level of enthusiasm and commitment to their own company and products and to serving their customers is going to be a key determinant of whether or not they become leaders in their field.

Leaders also empower others through encouragement. When you study the leadership stories of George Washington at Valley Forge encouraging his soldiers, Napoleon marching with his soldiers into battle, and Alexander the Great camping with his troops in the field and telling his troops how much he believed in them, you know that encouragement is a powerful tool in inspiring and motivating.

Leaders inspire trust and confidence. The wonderful thing is that if we truly believe in our leadership and the people who are in charge, we will do things that are far beyond anything we can imagine. If our trust or our confidence in those people wanes, then our motivation suffers.

Finally, leaders inspire loyalty, and loyalty, as you know, is the cement that binds together an organization. Loyalty is actually critical and vital to the success of any organization. Leaders get people to become totally loyal and dedicated to the organization.

SEVEN

Commit to Winning

HOW DO LEADERS get followers? What is it that enables average men and women to elicit extraordinary performance from average people? Why do people confer the title of leader on an individual? One simple reason: People are made leaders because they are seen to be the individuals who are most likely to lead the organization to victory. Leadership equals winning.

The main task of leadership is victory. That's why when companies are underperforming or when the team is losing, the very first thing they do is replace the CEO or the coach with someone they believe can lead them to victory. Your ability to lead people to victory and instill the belief that your team can win is the key to cinching your power as a leader.

Leaders are committed to excellence and quality, because excellence and quality lead to winning. When you go into the marketplace with your product or service, one thing your people like to know is that they are representing the best. Quality and service are very important.

Leaders believe that their organizations are capable of being the best in their field. And their aim is to make their organization superior—number one, top of the heap, the best. Not just as good as someone else or not quite as bad as someone else, but the best.

Finally, leaders think in terms of success. They think success all the time. If we think about success all the time, then it is inevitable that we will be successful. If individuals within your organization think of success, whether in terms of increasing sales and profitability, lowering costs, or prosperity and success in the marketplace, then they will become successful, too.

Lessons from Military Strategy

A military leader has but one goal: victory. Many business leaders find inspiration and guidance from military leaders and military strategy. As I wrote in my book *Victory!*, I have found that the principles of military strategy can lead to victory in any field. Here are those principles.

■ *The Principle of the Objective.* Military leaders are perfectly clear on the goal(s) of the operation. There can be no fuzziness on this point. For business, the same clarity and commitment is necessary. Your employees, every one of them, must know what they must do and be as committed to victory as soldiers on the battlefield.

▪ *The Principle of the Offensive.* Napoleon said, "No great battles are ever won on the defensive." Leaders don't play it safe; they don't wait to see what happens. They go out and take control of the situation. Without being foolhardy, they are aggressive and focused.

▪ *The Principle of the Mass.* This is a question of concentrating your forces—which in business means your best people, your best energies, and any resources that you have—on where you have the best chance for the greatest victory. Turnaround leaders often restructure activities to refocus the best talent of the organization on the results that can take the company out of its losing situation.

▪ *The Principle of Maneuver.* Most battlefield victories come from commanders who have outmaneuvered the enemy, often by attacking from the flank or the rear. Off the battlefield, the principle of maneuver translates into creativity and flexibility. As an example, perhaps it means doing the exact opposite of what you are doing now in order to turn a losing organization into a winner.

▪ *The Principle of Intelligence.* Leaders get the facts. They know that information is power. Obtain all the information you need to make the right decisions.

▪ *The Principle of Concerted Action.* Victory is achieved when everyone on the team is driven by shared goals and values. Everyone knows what the others are doing and why. Everyone trusts that the whole team is committed to the goal.

■ *The Principle of Unity of Command.* In any military operation, there needs to be one leader, one person who is ultimately responsible for the success of the operation. That applies to nonmilitary endeavors as well, especially during a crisis, when time is of the essence. Leaders make it clear in such situations that they are in charge and calling the shots.

EIGHT

The Leader as Communicator

LEADERS ARE excellent communicators. The ability to communicate is a core quality of leadership. That's because 85 percent of your success as a leader is determined by your ability to communicate effectively with others. After all, being a leader is about dealing with others—their success is your success. If you cannot communicate, you cannot be a leader.

Communication is a skill that can be learned. The first step is to understand the five goals that you want to accomplish through your communication:

1. *You want people to like and respect you.* Leadership is not about making friends, but if you are liked and respected, people will be more willing to listen to you. They will want to hear what you have to say.

2. *You want people to recognize your value and importance.* The objective, again, is to give people a reason to listen to you.

3. *You want to be able to persuade others to accept your view.* Leadership today is more about persuasion than commanding. You have to be able to persuade others to see your point of view and agree with your position.

4. *You want to get people to change their minds and to cooperate with you.* You cannot be a successful leader if you have people who are against you or who refuse to change their previous positions and opinions. Leaders are often change agents, and the key to change is effective communication.

5. *You want to be more influential overall in your relationships.* Leadership is about power and influence, and power and influence is best achieved through effective communication.

Be Clear

Leaders articulate their views, their strategies, and their visions with clarity. Wherever you find an organization that's drifting, you find a fuzzy understanding of the reason behind the organization. In a successful organization, employees at all levels know with crystal clarity what it is they are trying to accomplish, where they are going, and what their future is. They know, with clarity, what their strengths and weaknesses are.

If you want to be a great leader, learn how to express your views, ideas, and goals clearly to other people. And make sure that those people who are expected to help know what they are expected to contribute.

Set Expectations

The number one complaint of employees in the workplace today is not knowing what is expected of them. It is amazing how many people are on payrolls, expected to contribute to the achievement of the goals of the organization, but are unsure about what they should be doing. People who don't clearly understand what they're supposed to be doing become negative and cynical, engage in politics, and become demotivated and incapable of making their maximum contribution to the organization.

In addition to the "what," leaders also communicate the reasons "why." As much as anything else, leaders make sure people know why they are doing what they are doing. Every one of us in today's workforce needs to know why we are doing a job. It's not enough for us to be told that this job or task is what you are going to do; we want to know the reasons. We want to know how the work affects us. We want to know how it affects our customers and other people. Nietzsche wrote, "A man can bear any *what* if he has a big enough *why*."

Through the years, I have developed a habit of never asking anyone to write or type a letter for me without explaining to the person why. I have found that the more you tell people why, the more motivated, committed, loyal, dedicated, and involved they are in their work. The less they know about the why, the more indifferent they become.

You can release potential in others just by telling them why. It doesn't even have to be a good reason, but they just have to have one.

Always Be Visible

The best way to communicate with others is face-to-face. In person. If you look at the great generals and other great leaders, you will find that they are always in the field. Very seldom do you find them hiding behind desks. As a matter of fact, the further up you go on the managerial ladder, the more time the individual leader spends in the field actually talking with people.

In fact, the expression MBWA, which is management by wandering around, means to get out of the office, walk around, and talk to people about what they're doing. Be visible and approachable so that people will come to you and tell you their problems and what's going on in their departments. You will get more immediate and timely information by getting out among your staff and your customers than you could by spending hours, days, or even weeks in your office. The very best leaders are out of the office walking around, remaining visible and approachable and available to others about 50 percent of the time.

Visibility is especially important in communicating with and learning from customers. Leaders should spend a minimum of 25 percent of their time with customers—not sitting behind a desk or looking at numbers and statistics, but actually going out into the field and taking care of customers.

Not that long ago VCRs were very popular. There is a story of a gentleman who was buying a VCR in a computer and electronics store in Santa Clara and an old Japanese man who served him across the counter. His English was quite poor. As the customer was leaving the store with his purchase, a friend of his pulled him aside and said, "Do you know who that was?" "No," the man replied. "That is Akio Morita, the head of Sony Corporation." Morita was traveling in the United States, visiting stores, and actually selling products to get feedback from the customers.

Always Be Selling

One final point about communication: Leaders are excellent low-pressure salespeople. Leaders are always selling. They are selling people on the organization, on the vision, on the goals, and on the reasons. They are selling people on working longer, harder hours, making more valuable contributions, coming on board, and taking greater responsibility. All great leaders can sell.

In addition to being able to sell, leaders can negotiate, and they can compromise. They have the capacity to find win-win solutions. It is a key part of leadership to take people with different points of view, different needs, and different attitudes, and harmonize those points of view so that they all work together in cooperation to achieve the goals of the organization.

Learn from Adversity

LEADERS NEVER use the word *failure*. They never think in terms of failure. They recognize valuable lessons, learning experiences, and temporary setbacks, but they never think in terms of failure. Inspirational author Orison Swett Marden wrote, "There is no failure for the man who realizes his power, who never knows when he is beaten; there is no failure for the determined endeavor; the unconquerable will. There is no failure for the man who gets up every time he falls, who rebounds like a rubber ball, who persists when everyone else gives up, who pushes on when everyone else turns back."

Thomas J. Watson of IBM was asked by a young executive many years ago, "How can I move ahead more rapidly in my career?" Watson's reply was, "Double your failure rate." In other words, the more often you fail and learn, the more rapidly you'll succeed.

Some leaders even say things like, "We have to fail faster around here if we want to succeed in our market." In other words, we have to gain our lessons quicker. Instead of one or two failures a year, experience ten or twenty failures and you'll be more likely to be in a position, knowledgewise, to dominate your market.

Be Solution-Oriented

Leaders can deal with setbacks and crises because they are solution-oriented. If there is a problem, then they are thinking about how to deal with it, not about finding the person to blame.

In my book *Crunch Point*, I describe some of the important steps that leaders take to respond to a crisis or a setback, no matter how big:

- *Stay calm.* Refuse to worry or become angry. Of course, that's easier said than done, but leaders maintain their calm and their mental clarity because they are able to avoid becoming angry at something that they cannot change.

- *Be confident in your abilities.* You have handled crises in the past, and you will do it again.

- *Dare to go forward.* Don't be paralyzed by the sudden turn of events. Take specific actions immediately to remedy the situation.

- *Get the facts.* Find out exactly what happened before you make a decision.

- *Take control.* Accept 100 percent responsibility. Finding blame or dwelling on the past resolves nothing.

- *Cut your losses.* Walk away from a solution that can't be saved.

- *Manage the crisis.* Take charge, make a plan, and get busy resolving the problem.

- *Communicate constantly.* Keep people informed. Uncertainty compounds the crisis.

- *Identify your constraints.* Identify the limiting constraint that slows the resolution of the crisis and deal with it.

- *Unleash your creativity.* Develop as many solutions as possible.

- *Counterattack.* Assess the situation, get the facts, then go on the offensive.

- *Keep things simple.* In a crisis situation, there may be too much going on and too much to do. Focus on the most important jobs only.

- *Never compromise your integrity.* No matter what crisis or challenge you face, you must resolve it without ever compromising your integrity. Remember, everyone is watching.

- *Persist until you succeed.* No matter how difficult resolving a crisis may become or how long it takes, never give up.

The Turnaround Artists

Much leadership is situational. Many leaders rise to the fore because of a situation. I've seen men and women who've gone on for many years in average positions and then, because of a period of turbulence or adversity, they suddenly have leadership thrust upon them.

I've also seen people who have been excellent leaders in one situation and turned out to be poor leaders in another situation. Some people are very good leaders under stable conditions, and others are excellent under turbulent conditions.

Today in America, sometimes a business leader must act as a "turnaround artist." The turnaround artist is outstanding in situations where a company is in danger of collapsing because of serious problems with finances and changes in the marketplace. These leaders can reorganize and get the company back on track, sometimes in a matter of a few weeks, when all the efforts of existing leadership cannot get the job done.

So leadership is highly situational, but it is adversity that brings out great leaders. It is adversity that proves whether or not a leader is great. So whenever you find yourself facing an adverse situation, think of it as an opportunity for you to demonstrate that you have "the right stuff"—that you have what is necessary to be a leader.

Adversity draws out the true leaders. Epictetus wrote, "Circumstances do not make the man; they only reveal him to himself." It's in the hard times that true leaders stand out.

TEN

Build a Championship Team

WHEN WE TALK about leaders being made and not born, one of the things that we know is that the number one quality that puts you on the fast track to the executive suite, or puts your outfit at the top of its field, is the ability to put together a championship team. It is the ability to put together a group of men and women who can work together in harmony to accomplish great things.

Here are seven keys to building winning teams:

1. *Clear Coaching and Leadership.* Everybody knows who calls the shots. There is a coach, and everybody knows who the boss is. Winning leaders surround themselves with good people. You can tell the quality of the leader by the quality of the people the leader picks to surround himself with. Strong leaders always pick people that are better than them. Weak leaders will try to pick people who are weaker than they are.

2. *Intensive People Development and Training Focus.* To build a winning team, the entire focus internally has to be on building, motivating, encouraging, training, and upgrading the skills and abilities of your people.

3. *Heavy Emphasis on Planning.* This means one critical thing: Get the facts. In Harold Geneen's great book on managing, he writes that the key is facts. Don't be satisfied with the assumed facts or the hoped-for facts or the possible facts, but the real ones. Geneen writes that the facts don't lie, and the ability to plan well depends on market intelligence. If you look at a winning team or a winning general, what you find is that great battles are won because people on the winning side have good intelligence. They get accurate information and incorporate it into their planning. World War II may have been decided by the ability of the British to decrypt the German cipher machine, which allowed the British to translate secret messages going back and forth between enemy headquarters and the commanders in the field.

Also develop fallback plans. One of the characteristics of all great generals is that when they go into battle, no matter what the circumstances, they always ask themselves what they would do if they had to withdraw. At the Battle of Waterloo, Wellington held 17,000 veteran troops in reserve to cover his retreat should he lose the battle and be forced to withdraw. Even though he was almost defeated on the day of the battle, he never deployed those reserves. If he had, Wellington might have won earlier in the day and not have come so close to defeat. But an excellent general always has a fallback plan for the worst possible outcome. A leader who initiates a plan with no thought of what might go wrong is invariably one who will make a fatal mistake in business.

4. *Selective Assignments.* As a leader, you hire good people and you put them in assignments where they can make a major contribution. If they can't do well in that position, you move them around and keep rotating them until you find a place where they can make that valuable contribution.

5. *Ability to Weed Out Incompetents.* If the people you've selected cannot make a contribution, you must get rid of them. Because the longer you keep incompetent people, the more you look like an incompetent leader. Not only that, but you send a signal that there is a reward for being incompetent in this organization, and it's called job security. This situation demotivates others and causes them to contribute less than they are capable of contributing.

6. *Better Communication.* One of the biggest weaknesses in any organization is poor communication. There is not enough information flowing up, down, and sideways. Championship teams need open communications so that people can get information anywhere they want in the organization very quickly.

7. *Committing to Excellence.* A commitment to excellence is the only thing that really motivates people. Being the best gets them out of bed in the morning, excited and dedicated. That's why leaders are always talking in terms of winning, success, and being better than the others.

ELEVEN

Focus on Results

LEADERS ARE results-oriented rather than activities-oriented. Just doing something is worthless if what you're doing doesn't lead to a valuable result. Leaders are always thinking in terms of the results that are expected of them.

Getting results depends on asking yourself four questions over and over again:

1. *What are my high-value activities?* What are the things you do that contribute the greatest value to your work and your organization? These are the activities on which you should be focusing.

2. *What are my key result areas?* There are seldom more than five to seven key result areas for any position in an organization. These are the areas

where you absolutely have to get excellent results to fulfill your responsibilities. Once you've identified your key result areas, you have to set the highest standards of performance and meet those standards: Remember that others are watching you.

3. *What can I (and only I) do that, if done well, will make a real difference to my company?* You have responsibilities and tasks that you and only you must do; if you don't do them, they don't get done.

4. *What is the most valuable use of my time?* This is the key question. There are tasks that only you can get done, but too many leaders are not fulfilling their responsibilities because they have been pulled into other responsibilities and tasks that they should not be covering. The best leaders know what they are being paid for—and what they are *not* being paid to do.

Set Priorities

One of the key skills to getting results is to know how to set priorities. It's not enough to identify your high-value activities. Leaders prioritize ruthlessly so that that they are working on only the most important, highest-value activities.

One of the most effective methods to prioritize your tasks is to use the ABCDE method. This method requires you to list your tasks and give them a priority rating.

An "A" task is something important, something that you must do. If you don't do this task, there are going to be significant consequences. You will have more than one A task. In that case, label them as A-1, A-2, A-3, and so forth. A-1, of course, is the most important task of them all, with A-2 next.

A "B" task is one that should be done, and leaving it undone will also lead to consequences. However, the consequences aren't as bad or as dangerous as the consequences for an A-level task left undone. Never work on a B task when there's an A task yet to do.

A "C" task is something that would be nice to do, but for which there are no consequences. Reading a magazine or newspaper might be enjoyable and lets you keep up with politics or sports, but this is not a task that will make any contribution to your work. Never work on a C task when there's a B task left undone.

A "D" task is anything that you can delegate to someone else. One of the important leadership rules is that you should delegate to others anything that can be delegated. You have enough work that only you can do; you should not be spending your time on tasks that can be done by others. Ask yourself, "What can I and only I do that will make a major difference to the company?" If a task doesn't fall into this category, give it to someone else. The priority rule continues: Never work on a D task when there's a C task left undone.

An "E" task is something that needs to be eliminated. It shouldn't even be on the table. It has no consequences and is of no use. Perhaps it was a task that was important in the past but is now obsolete. Or perhaps it should have never been done at all! At any rate, now is the time to eliminate it.

The key to making this ABCDE method work is to never work on a lower-priority task when there is a higher task still undone. I emphasize this rule for each task, because it is easy to say but harder to remember or to do.

Focus Everyone on Effectiveness

At the same time that they are focused on their own results, leaders are always conveying to others what their key result areas are and motivating others to set priorities on high-payoff tasks. Leaders know that the ability to set priorities and to focus where you can make a significant difference is the key to human effectiveness, just as it is the key to the effectiveness of an organization and a leader.

If you are doing things that are not in your key result areas and you do them brilliantly, the outcomes will be worthless. But if you do one or two high-priority things really well, you can make an enormous and significant contribution.

TWELVE

The Desire to Lead

LEADERS HAVE an intense desire to lead. This is what is called the royal jelly or the fire in the belly. And what is absolutely necessary here is self-reliance. Interestingly enough, leaders tend to be very individualistic. They tend to be autonomous with a high need for control. They like to make their own decisions.

However, they also recognize that in order to get to the position where they can have control and autonomy, they have to be good followers. They have to follow orders meticulously. All great generals started off in boot camp learning how to be good followers of orders.

Leaders like to take command. They love to be in control and to take charge. Now, many people don't want to be leaders and not everybody needs to be a leader. But if you are meant for leadership, you have a tremendous desire and urge to take control, and your job is to prepare yourself to assume leadership responsibilities.

Take on the Responsibilities of Leadership

A leader has seven key responsibilities that never change in any situation or organization. Those who want to lead work hard at becoming the best in all seven of these areas.

Responsibility 1: Set and achieve goals. The best leaders have identified what needs to be accomplished in every area of importance to the organization and are able to achieve each of those goals. For business, that means setting sales growth and profitability goals and then leaving no part of the business untouched in the strategic and market planning to reach those goals.

Responsibility 2: Innovate and market. Don't keep doing what you or the organization have been doing all along. That's not the way you are going to get new customers. That's not the way you are going to achieve those goals that you embraced in the first responsibility. Innovate, and then sell—sell what you do, and sell what you've created.

Responsibility 3: Solve problems and make decisions. It is up to you to overcome setbacks, to hurdle the barriers on the path to success, and to make the difficult decisions that come with the position. Every unachieved goal is a problem unsolved. If you did not reach your sales targets, that's a problem unsolved. If you are still getting beat in your market, that's a problem unsolved.

Responsibility 4: Set priorities and focus on key tasks. No leader has unlimited people, money, or any other kind of resource. It is the job of the leader to know how to deploy the resources of the organization in the way that best contributes to the overall success of the organization. The fourth responsibility is also about time management. Time is the scarcest resource of all, and leaders who don't know how to allocate their time will fail.

Responsibility 5: Be a role model to others. People watch their leaders and emulate their behaviors and attitudes. Through your character, personality, and work habits, you must set the example that you want to see in others.

Responsibility 6: Persuade and inspire others to follow you. Leaders motivate their teams, their departments, or their organizations to believe in the vision, mission, and specific goals that they have set for the organization. A leader without followers is not a leader, no matter what his or her position may be.

Responsibility 7: Get results. Leaders are expected to perform. There are no excuses. There are no acceptable reasons for not achieving results. The seventh responsibility is the most critical responsibility of all.

Like an athlete who wants the ball, a leader embraces these responsibilities. Leaders want to be held accountable;

they want to be responsible for motivating the people in the organization and achieving the results required for success. Leaders recognize that success comes from a partnership with their people, but ultimately, they want to be the ones in command.

Be Ready to Be Accountable

Those who want to lead know that they will be held accountable for results, and they want to be responsible for results. They want to be held accountable for the success of the organization. And if something goes wrong, they are ready to accept the blame.

As a leader, refuse to criticize others for any reason. Refuse to complain about your situation. Erase the phrases "what if" and "if only" from your vocabulary. Focus on what you want and where you are going. And if there is something that needs to be fixed, take responsibility for fixing it.

Accepting accountability is the reason that leaders feel personally powerful. They have a sense of control over themselves and their lives. Accepting responsibility gives them confidence and energy. They feel capable and competent.

Those who make excuses, blame others, or complain give their power away. They weaken themselves and their resolve. They convince themselves that they have no control over what happens. Leaders believe that they have the control in their hands—otherwise, they could not be leaders. They could only be passive and resigned rather than taking the initiative.

Even leaders within a large corporation have a self-employed attitude. They believe that they are the president of their own personal service corporation. They have an entrepreneurial attitude. This entrepreneurial attitude emphasizes their sense of responsibility and accountability.

Now Is the Right Time

When you have the desire to lead, you don't let outside circumstances slow you down. That's why those who have the fire of leadership in them don't wait for the "right time." The right time is now. Some of the greatest companies in the world were created during times of economic hardship. Walt Disney, Bill Hewlett and David Packard, and IBM's Tom Watson are just some of the leaders who launched their great companies in some of America's worst economic crises. Companies as diverse as FedEx, Hyatt, MTV, and Trader Joe's were all started during recessions.

Remember, there will never be too many leaders. There will never be more leaders than are necessary. There is always a shortage of leaders. Do you have the desire to lead?

THIRTEEN

The Role of Self-Esteem in Leadership

LEADERS HAVE high self-esteem and a positive self-image. They value themselves and feel worthwhile.

Self-esteem is simply how much you like yourself. An important part of self-esteem is self-efficacy. It is a feeling of competence, of being good at what you do, and being capable of achieving the results you need to achieve as a leader.

Self-esteem is important because the way you feel *inside*, the beliefs and ideas that you have about yourself, is going to guide the way you perform on the *outside*. According to Steve Rodgers, the former CEO of Prudential Bache California Realty, "The way you feel about yourself has everything to do with how you perform as an individual in your own work and as a manager of people."

Being a leader requires calm, clarity, persistence, the ability to see the world as it truly is, and many other qualities that are impossible if the leader is wrestling with self-doubt and feelings of inferiority.

The Keys to High Self-Esteem

Leaders know themselves. Like the Delphic Oracle, they have a very high level of *self-awareness*. They take a good deal of time for introspection; they know what makes them tick. They know their own motives and why they do what they do. They are also capable of being very objective with themselves rather than overly emotionally involved. In other words, they have low egos but high pride.

They also only take on tasks that they can perform at an excellent level. Because they know themselves, they will not take on a job, task, or assignment where they do not have the ability to do it extremely well. They know that everything they do contributes to their overall image as a leader, so they will only take on things they can do well.

They focus on their unique strengths and ask, "Is this the sort of thing I can excel at and have the qualities and abilities to perform exceptionally?" And if they can't perform exceptionally, they'll back off. They are always looking for superior results and not just average results.

They also have *self-honesty*. They evaluate themselves honestly. They are not arrogant or prideful or vain or boastful. They have the ability to look into themselves and ask, "Is this right for me? Is this the right step for me to be taking at this time?"

How Do You Treat Others?

Leaders with high self-esteem are nondefensive. They are secure enough to learn from mistakes and deal with setbacks. A nonleader will not have the inner strength to overcome mistakes or confront adversity.

Nor will nonleaders have the self-esteem to recognize that they have both strengths and weaknesses. Leaders recognize their areas of strengths but have also identified their weaknesses and set about to overcome them. There is a difference between whining about weaknesses and dealing with them calmly and honestly. That difference comes from self-esteem. Leaders recognize that they are not perfect, but know that they are still competent and skilled.

One sign of people with low self-esteem is in the way they treat others. People with low self-esteem will overcompensate by treating others poorly, just to make themselves feel better. Effective leaders treat everyone, the weak and the powerful, the same way. Richard Branson, the charismatic founder of the Virgin Group, once disguised himself as a limo driver for a television series based on *The Apprentice.* He then watched to see how the entrepreneurs being tested on the show treated him. Those who treated him poorly were fired. They did not have what it takes to be an effective leader.

Believe in Yourself

Self-esteem begins with being good at what you do. Leaders commit themselves to excellent performance. They will accept nothing else from themselves or others. They want to be in the top 10 percent of their field.

Achieving high levels of performance is the way that people with low self-esteem can escape the trap of low self-esteem. It begins with realizing that anything is possible. I came from a poor background with few opportunities, and because of this background, I suffered from low self-esteem that held me back. Even if I did something well, I refused to take credit, passing it off to luck or coincidence. It wasn't until I was twenty-eight that I had a revelation that changed my life. This revelation was that every single person in the top 10 percent of his or her field had to start somewhere, and that somewhere was often in the bottom 10 percent. Everyone doing well today was once doing poorly.

From that point, I took responsibility for developing myself. I realized that life is a self-serve buffet line, and it was up to me to get up, accept responsibility, and "serve" myself. There are two steps necessary to get to the front of the buffet line: First, get in line, and second, stay in line. Getting in line means making the decision to improve yourself, every day, working toward your goals. Staying in line means not giving up, not making a short-lived attempt at improving yourself and then going back to watching television and being a victim.

When Bob Silver went to one of my seminars in Chicago, he was twice divorced, overweight, unemployed, and deep in debt. He believed that all his problems were caused by others or by fate. Life was unfair, and that's all there was to it.

He came to my seminar at the insistence of a friend, but he wasn't happy to be there because he didn't believe in all that "motivational stuff." But when I said that nature was neutral, and that you are what you are because of yourself and nothing else, Bob Silver suddenly realized that he, not life, was the problem. He was holding himself back because of his attitude, because of his focus on what he didn't have instead of what he wanted. From that point on he decided to change his life, and within one year, he was employed and had been promoted twice, he had lost thirty pounds, and he was happily remarried. High self-esteem can turn your life around.

High self-esteem means believing in yourself. It will give you the persistence and focus to stay in line.

FOURTEEN

Lead by Example

WHEN YOU ARE a leader, everybody is watching what you are doing and what you are saying. Your behavior will guide the behavior of the other members of your team or the people in your organization. You set the example, and they will follow that example. Albert Schweitzer said, "You must teach men at the school of example, for they will learn at no other." Marshall Goldsmith, one of the world's top executive coaches, has shown through his work that changing a single behavioral characteristic in a leader can have a deep impact on the behavior of a very large number of people.

Let's examine a few of the characteristics and traits that people will closely observe in their leaders and base their behavior on.

Never Cheat

Never lie or cheat, take shortcuts, or take advantage of your position. Take responsibility for your actions. When you are in a position of power, it may be easy to blame others for poor results. No one will argue with you because people want to keep their jobs. But they will know. They will have observed your behavior, and they will no longer feel it necessary to act with integrity themselves. When a scandal takes down a company such as Enron, it is because the leadership created a culture of cheating in the organization that filtered down to all levels. The expression "The fish stinks from the head down" refers to this top-down effect. If you aren't a role model of integrity and character, you could be sowing the seeds of your company's eventual destruction. If, on the other hand, you never compromise on your integrity, your employees and the other leaders in the organization will go the extra mile to match your integrity and character.

Have the Right Attitude

Leaders generally have a positive and optimistic attitude. They believe strongly in themselves and their organization, and they don't let setbacks or barriers get them down. Attitude goes a long way in overcoming adversity, and one of the best ways of helping your people overcome any problems or hurdles that they may be facing in their jobs is to model your optimism. By watching the way in which you deal with adversity, they will find the strength to fight back.

In his bestselling book *Learned Optimism*, University of Pennsylvania professor Martin Seligman used results from

350,000 interviews to prove that successful people are much more optimistic than people who have mediocre or no success. He found that optimism was the defining characteristic of successful people, more than any other personality or behavioral trait. Optimism is important because it focuses your thoughts on what can be done in the future to make things better, not on what happened in the past to make things worse.

Even if, deep inside, you might have some doubts or uncertainties, those doubts must stay hidden from the people who look up to you. The best leaders do not allow themselves the luxury of discussing their doubts or uncertainties with others. There is nothing more demoralizing than to see your leader expressing self-doubt. Not only will self-doubt in a leader hurt morale, but it will also raise a question in people's minds about whether you are up to the task. Once your leadership is questioned, you will lose the trust of your people and you will become an ineffective leader. That is why leading by example is essential to your success as a leader.

Treat Others with Respect

Another element of attitude is the way a leader treats others. People will know how you treat them and will see how you treat their colleagues, their bosses, or even the organization's customers and partners, and they will follow your example. Leaders know that if they are rude to a customer, their people will be rude to customers, and their business will acquire a reputation that will keep customers away. They know that if they do not treat their managers with respect and civility, those managers won't treat their own subordinates with respect and civility, and the business will acquire a reputation for mistreating employees, which will keep the best people away.

Leaders also know that if they act as yes people to their own superiors, such as the board of directors, then they will find themselves surrounded by yes people as well, instead of honest collaborators who will give them the facts they need to help the organization succeed.

How you treat others sets the tone for your team or your organization. As a leader, it is up to you to set the right tone.

Model Good Work Habits

Another example that you must set is in your work habits. The best leaders work hard and work long, and this behavior inspires others to do the same. Leaders who take advantage of their position to come in late and leave early, or who are seen frequently socializing with managers or employees, will find that the productivity of their team, department, or organization becomes lower and lower.

Leaders are excellent role models. They strive to continually set a good example in their behavior and in their conduct. They are aware that others are observing them and are aware of their effect on the morale and conduct of their people. Remember: There are no bad soldiers under a good general.

That's why it is important to ask yourself: "What kind of a company would my company be if everyone in it was just like me?"

FIFTEEN

Self-Motivation for Leaders

LEADERS TAKE responsibility for keeping themselves motivated. They meet this responsibility using three methods. One is through their vision.

Most real leaders, especially transformational leaders who have the ability to create the future, are dreamers. They dream of a future and of possibilities that nobody has thought of before. Sometimes a true leader can see a future with crystal clarity while other people around them cannot imagine it at all. Then the leaders go forward, and through planning, administering, and organizing, they make their dreams come true.

When I conduct strategic planning exercises with corporations, I ask the gathered leaders to imagine a future where in five years the company was the very best in its industry. Once everyone has developed the ideal features and attributes of this future ideal company, I ask, "Is this possible?" One by one, the executives will begin to nod and say, "Yes, it is possible. Maybe not in one year, but in five years, yes." We then discuss how to reach that ideal over the next five years. Once you have a clear vision of what you want, the next question is always "How?"

You can practice this same exercise for your life. Imagine that you have no limitations—no limitations of money, education, experience, contacts, or anything else. Now imagine your ideal life in five years. What are you doing? What does your life look like? Once you have the details of your dream, the next step is to make it happen. Think about what you have to start doing today to achieve your "five-year fantasy." The great Peter Drucker wrote, "We greatly overestimate what we can do in one year. But we greatly underestimate what is possible for us in five years."

Set Goals and Gain Commitment

Second, leaders motivate themselves continually by setting higher goals. We know that if you keep setting higher and higher goals, if you keep striving and make sure your reach exceeds your grasp, you will stay motivated.

And, finally, leaders motivate themselves by gaining the commitment of others. What leaders find is that when other people will commit to the dream, it in turn makes them more enthusiastic and more dedicated. The employees of Zappos.com are committed to CEO Tony Hsieh's dream of the ultimate customer service experience. How does he know? Because at the end of customer service training, new

Zappos employees are offered a $2,000 check to leave. It may seem like a strange proposition, but the goal is simple: to make sure that the employees who stay really want to be there and are committed to the ideals of the company. A tiny fraction of new employees grab the money and run—which is just as well, because they would probably never be as committed as those who turn their backs on easy money for a chance to work for Zappos.

Work Hard

Success does not come easy. Leaders are self-motivated to put in the work required to achieve their dreams. As a consequence:

- *Leaders work harder.* The workplace is not the place to socialize. It is not the place to wander around the Internet. Leaders don't waste time when they are in the workplace.

- *Leaders work faster.* They are always looking to pick up the pace, immediately. They are never satisfied with their speed. They want to get more done, faster.

- *Leaders work longer hours.* Most leaders are the first ones in the office. And they are often the last to leave. Just those extra hours a week make a huge difference in their productivity.

Leaders are at the top of the pole. They cannot depend on others to motivate them; they have to be self-motivating. Of course, being a leader is a very motivating experience in itself.

SIXTEEN

Develop Leadership Qualities

LEADERS NEVER stop growing and developing. As a matter of fact, in one of the most extensive studies of leaders done in the last couple of decades, what we have found is that true leaders have the capacity to grow and develop and keep themselves from falling into a comfort zone. They are lifelong students.

Read and Study

A key to developing leadership qualities is to read, study, and take courses. All leaders are readers. Even though they are swamped with work, they never stop taking in new information. They never stop reading business books and magazines, attending conferences, getting into discussions, and learning what is going on.

George Washington was born into a middle-class family with few advantages and eventually became the commander of the United States military forces and the first president of the United States. During the turbulent times of the founding of our nation, Washington was known for always being gracious and correct in his manner and behavior. What few people realize is that a book he read when he was a teenager helped guide his behavior throughout his long and storied life. The book was called *The Rules of Civility and Decent Behavior in Company and Conversation*. Washington wrote down the book's 110 rules in a personal notebook and would keep it with him for the rest of his life.

Many leaders read biographies and autobiographies of other leaders because they are looking for role models to serve as examples for their lives. David McClelland of Harvard University researched the effect of role models on shaping the character and the personality of young people. As he explained in his book *The Achieving Society*, the men and women that society holds up as role models during a person's youth will have a major impact on the character of that person for the rest of his or her life. Those who become great leaders, however, go beyond the current role models of society; they seek out the best leaders from history through reading and study.

Work on the Qualities You're Missing

People will be born with certain leadership qualities but missing others. Most great leaders became great because they identified the leadership qualities that they were missing and then deliberately set out to acquire those skills.

Benjamin Franklin, another one of our founding fathers, also worked hard at developing the qualities he thought he needed as a leader. Franklin believed that he was too rough around the edges, too argumentative and ill-mannered, to be successful. So he deliberately set out to change his personality. He sat down and wrote a list of thirteen virtues that he believed he needed to possess. And then he began learning to act according to those virtues. Every week he would choose one virtue to focus on, such as tolerance or tranquility. But Franklin knew, as did Washington, that leadership qualities are not acquired in just a week. Franklin continued to study the virtues, eventually focusing on a specific virtue for a period of two weeks, then three weeks, then a month. The once rough and off-putting Franklin became one of the most influential diplomats working on behalf of our fledgling nation. His diplomacy in Paris was vital in acquiring the international allies the colonists would need to defeat a nation as powerful as England. And it all began with sitting down and working on thirteen virtues.

As you are working to make yourself better, remember these three rules:

- *It doesn't matter where you came from.* It only matters where you are going. Don't worry about any past opportunities that you may have missed or any mistakes you may have made because of a weakness. That is all past. It is the future that counts. Just because you haven't been a leader before doesn't mean you can't become one.

- *If you want your life to get better, you have to get better.* That's what this chapter is about. If you want to be a leader, then you need to develop your leadership qualities.

- *You can learn anything that you want to learn.* You can become anything you want to become. Leaders such as Benjamin Franklin knew what they wanted to be and then set about making it happen.

Become a Better Leader

Leaders are always looking to improve themselves. In four basic steps, you can improve your leadership skills and qualities:

1. *Do more of certain things.* Do more of those things that are of greater value to you and more important to achieving your results as a leader.

2. *Do less of certain things.* At the same time, you must deliberately decide to reduce the amount of time you spend on certain activities that impede your success as a leader.

3. *Start to do those things you aren't doing that you need to be doing.* What are the skills, competencies,

or knowledge that you need in order to succeed as a leader? Identify them, and then either acquire them or learn them.

4. *Stop doing certain things altogether.* There may be activities that are no longer relevant to your goals as a leader. Step back and evaluate all your activities from the perspective of what you are trying to achieve. You may find that what was once important is no longer important and should no longer take up your time.

SEVENTEEN

Power Through Cooperation

LEADERS RECOGNIZE that they can't do it all themselves, so they are always alert to enlisting competent men and women who can help them achieve their goals. Leaders recognize that the greatest single limitation in any endeavor in human society is talented people. So leaders are always seeking out talented people, one way or another.

Seek out the advice of others. One of the most important rules of success I ever heard is that you need to ask your way to success. Ask other people for the help you need. Ask for advice. Ask for counsel. Never assume that you know it all or try to learn it from the ground up. As they say, you'll never live long enough to make every mistake. So ask others and learn from them.

Also, compensate for weaknesses. Be very alert to your weaknesses and figure out how to compensate for them. The fact of the matter is that if you can compensate for your weaknesses and build on your strengths, you can become an exceptional leader.

All leaders have peaks of tremendous strength and valleys where they are weak. Good leaders are able to find people who are strong where they are weak; that way they can concentrate on developing their own strengths to even greater heights. Don't worry about being weak in a few areas because it doesn't matter, as long as you bring along other talented people who can help you achieve your goals.

Steps to Cooperation

Here are three important steps to achieve power through cooperation. First of all, identify the key people in your life who can help you, whether you work with them or whether they work in parallel organizations. Identify these key people and think of how you can align yourself with them. One of the best and most powerful ways to get people to help you is to help them.

Second, take the time to develop relationships with these key people. Everything in life today is about relationships. Your success in life is going to be determined by the quality and quantity of successful relationships that you can form with other talented people.

Finally, make the effort to preserve and enhance those worthwhile relationships. One person who is in the right place at the right time and with whom you've developed a relationship over the years can save you five years of hard work.

Mastermind Groups

I recommend setting up mastermind groups. In San Diego, we established a mastermind group of entrepreneurs—successful entrepreneurs who meet regularly with other successful entrepreneurs to discuss new business ideas and also get feedback and advice on business problems or questions. In some cases, an entrepreneur who has been struggling with an issue for months may find a solution in minutes.

Mastermind groups can be structured or unstructured. In a structured group, there may be a brainstorming session around an assigned topic or question. Members of the group will often be exposed to new ideas or perspectives that they can apply to their businesses. In unstructured groups, the members simply get together and discuss whatever topics they might be preoccupied with.

A mastermind group doesn't have to be external. As a leader, you should develop a mastermind group of key people in your own business or organization to meet with regularly in order to get a general sense of how business is going and what problems are coming up.

Managed Dependencies

Power entails managed dependencies. Power is having people who are loyal to you and that you can count on for favors, even though they are not subordinate to you in any way.

Often, these people are ready to help you because you have helped them. It's called the Law of Reciprocity. The Law of Reciprocity says that if you do things to help other people achieve their goals, they will be compelled internally to do things to help you achieve your goals.

Likability is also a key to power and influence. People will always do more and better things for people that they like than they will for people that they don't like.

The Power of Mentorship

Most successful leaders had mentors who helped guide them to the top. Here's some advice on how to build better and more successful mentor-mentee relationships.

- Set clear goals for yourself in every area of your life. You won't know what type of people can help you until you know exactly what you want to accomplish.

- Identify the obstacles and roadblocks on the path to your goals.

- Identify the areas of knowledge, skill, and expertise you need to acquire to overcome these obstacles. This will tell you what you need to learn from your mentors.

- Look around you and select the most successful people in the areas where you will need the most help.

- Join the clubs, organizations, and business associations that these kinds of people belong to. It may take a little bit of research, but this information can be found.

- Once you've joined these clubs, organizations, and associations, become actively involved. Volunteering for assignments and taking on tasks will bring you to the attention of the kind of people you want to meet faster than anything else.

- Work, study, and practice continually to get better and better at what you do. To attract the best mentors, you need to develop a reputation for being an up-and-coming person in your field.

- When you find a potential mentor, remember that you are dealing with a very busy person. Don't make a nuisance of yourself. Instead, ask for ten minutes of the person's time, in private, to ask for advice. Nothing more.

- When you do meet with a potential mentor, explain that you want to be more successful in your field and would very much appreciate a little guidance and advice. Ask for an answer to a specific question, or a recommendation of a specific book or other resource, or a specific idea that the individual found helpful in the past.

- After the initial meeting, send a sincere thank-you note to the person. Mention that you hope that you can call the person again if you have another question.

- Each month, drop your mentor a short note about your progress and about what you are doing. Make it clear that you are listening to your mentor's advice. You are reading the recommended books, taking the recommended courses. There is nothing that makes a potential mentor more open to helping you than your making it clear that the help is doing some good.

- Arrange to meet with your mentor again, perhaps monthly or even more often, if you and the other person work closely together.

One final note: As you grow and develop through the course of your life and career, move on to mentors who can give you more and different and better advice relevant to where you are now.

EIGHTEEN

Lead by Consensus

LEADERS RULE three ways: by command, by consultation, or by consensus.

The traditional way of leading was by command. A leader gave orders and everyone was supposed to follow them. Today, leaders recognize that issuing orders without any consultation or without any explanation of why the orders are necessary is not a good way of getting people motivated to do their best. As Major General Gale Pollock (Ret.), the first woman surgeon general of the U.S. Army, explains: "If you order people to do something that they don't understand, they won't give it all they've got. The greatest performances and courage come when you show them why it matters."

The second way to lead is by consultation. The consultation decision is where you ask people for their advice and input, and then you make the decision. This is a more motivating way of leading others than through simple commands. People will realize that the final decision is yours, but they will appreciate the fact that they were consulted in the decision-making process. And even if they don't agree with the final decision, they will be more likely to abide by it because of this consultation.

Consensus goes even further in involving others in the decision making. In this case, a leader does not make the final decision; that final decision belongs 100 percent to the group. The group must discuss the pros and cons of every action and then finally agree on the action to take.

Leaders will use all three methods, and they make it clear when discussing a critical decision what kind of a decision it is. Not every decision is appropriate for a consensus decision or for a command decision. Although a consensus decision has advantages, it is not an excuse for the leader to abdicate responsibility. What's important is that people understand when something requires a consultative or a consensus decision and when it is a command decision.

Leaders are paid to make the difficult decisions, and sometimes that means issuing a command. Yet the best leaders also recognize that there is a direct link between ownership of an idea and the degree to which people participate in discussing the idea. Leaders realize that the more people can engage in dialogue about an idea, the more likely it is that they will be committed to the implementation of the idea.

Leaders avoid giving orders whenever possible. Leaders always encourage people to think about and talk about and discuss ideas because they know that the more involved people are, the more likely they will be committed to supporting the final decision.

Create the Right Environment

Leading by consultation or consensus requires a high-trust environment in which people are empowered and unafraid to tell the truth or to take responsibility. Here is how to create the right environment for consultation or consensus leadership.

RESPOND TO PROBLEMS QUICKLY

Nobody wants to do a bad job, but there will be problems. If any problem arises, deal with it quickly. Talk directly to the person involved and calmly seek out solutions to the problem. Don't blame, accuse, or pass judgment. There is a good chance the problem didn't originate with the employee, but rather with the company itself or a supervisor. Whatever the cause of the problem, discover it and find a solution.

HELP EMPLOYEES IMPROVE

Employees want a chance to improve. Create an environment that not only allows mistakes, but actually encourages employees to raise their performance levels. You can help employees improve through the following steps:

- *Clarify expectations from the very beginning.* Make sure that employees know exactly what results you expect from them. Make those results as objective as possible.

- *Set measurable standards of performance.* Remember that "what gets measured gets done." Put financial measures on each output.

- *Never assume that the employee has completely understood your instructions.* When you delegate an assignment or a project to your employees, make sure they are taking notes and then ask them to read back the assignment.

- *Give regular feedback.* Tell people what they are doing well and what they can change and improve. Feedback is motivating because it sends the message that you are interested in their work. Being in the dark about how well you might be doing is demotivating. Most of all, people love the feeling of a job well done. Let them know.

DEAL WITH PROBLEMS CALMLY

It is sometimes easy to become angry or impatient when a problem arises. Keep the attitude that despite the apparent problems, the employee had the best of intentions. Then deal with the problem calmly and in a way that does not humiliate the employee.

- Don't criticize the employee or discuss the problem in a public place. Call the employee into your office to talk about the situation.

- Be very specific about the problem or misunderstanding. Explain clearly why you are concerned.

■ Hear the employee out completely. Even if the employee becomes defensive, the employee's side of the situation might throw a completely different light on what happened.

■ If the employee is at fault, set clear expectations about how the employee's performance must improve and by how much. There is nothing more frustrating—and demotivating—than to be told to resolve a challenge or prevent a problem without being told how. People want to know exactly what they can do to fix the problem.

■ Follow up. Has the employee made the adjustments that were agreed upon? Offer feedback and additional support when necessary.

NINETEEN

Leaders Are Listeners

LEADERS ARE excellent listeners. As much as 50 percent to 60 percent of a leader's time is spent listening. The key to being an excellent listener is listening not only for the words, but for what is going on behind the words. Listen for the real message and focus all your attention on the person who is speaking. In meetings and in your conversions with others:

- *Listen attentively.* Clear your mind and focus on what the speaker is saying. Don't try to "fake it" because it won't work: People will know that your mind is elsewhere. Researchers have shown that in conversations, words themselves comprise only 7 percent of a message. The rest of the message is conveyed through your tone of voice (38 percent) and, most important, your body language, which accounts for 55 percent of the message. Physically adjust your body and adopt a listening posture, by leaning forward toward the speaker. This gesture sends a clear message to the speaker that you are listening. And don't interrupt. If you are talking, you are not listening.

▪ *Pause before replying.* When the speaker stops talking or there is a break in the discussion, you may be tempted to jump in, assuming that the other person is finished. However, the person may just be reorganizing his thoughts momentarily before continuing. Your interjection at this point will be seen as an interruption. If you pause before replying and allow a moment of silence, you allow yourself to hear the other person's meaning at a deeper level. You'll have a better chance to understand what other people are saying because you are not busy formulating your own thoughts while they are still speaking. Finally, pausing when the other person has finished speaking sends a message that you are really listening and that you are carefully considering what the person has said before you offer a reply.

▪ *Question for clarification.* Asking questions is another technique that proves that you were truly listening to what the speaker was saying and not just pretending to listen. Equally important, asking questions will prevent you from making the wrong assumptions or drawing the wrong conclusions about what the speaker was trying to say. Don't assume you understand if you are not sure. Drill down by asking questions such as:

"How do you mean, exactly?"

"How do you feel about that?"

Paraphrase what the speaker has said in your own words and repeat it back to the person. Not only will the speaker know you have been listening, but she will also know whether you have understood what she said. And if you have gotten something wrong, the speaker now has an opportunity to correct you.

- *Listen without interruptions.* During the Battle of Waterloo, Napoleon sent a message to Marshal Grouchy, who had 30,000 troops a short distance away from the battlefield. Because Napoleon had to send his message in haste, the orders that reached Grouchy were so confused that he did not know what to do and so did nothing. He sat there with 30,000 men while Napoleon was defeated at Waterloo just a few hills away and the entire course of European history was changed. And it was simply because of a lack of attentiveness to the message.

If you are a leader and a person wants to talk to you, close the door, turn off the telephones, and listen single-mindedly without interruption. Listening is one of the finest ways that you can learn what is going on. A casual attitude toward listening can be disastrous for you.

TWENTY

Live Like a Leader

LEADERS ARE active and productive and set the example for others by working hard and long. However, effective leaders also know that lifestyle choices can make a big difference in their success. Leaders take care of themselves physically, mentally, and emotionally, which gives them the energy and peace of mind to deal with the challenges and stress of leadership.

Here are some lifestyle rules that the best leaders follow:

- *Get lots of sleep.* With seven to eight hours of sleep, you will have more energy and be more alert, positive, and resilient. As a leader, you must be fully present at all times. You cannot allow yourself to be overtired or in any kind of a mental fog.

▪ *Recharge your batteries.* Times of challenge and crisis can be especially exhausting. Although it may seem unproductive, sometimes it is necessary to take a full day off from anything that has to do with the business.

▪ *Shut down completely.* Perhaps the best way to recharge your batteries is to shut down completely for thirty-six hours. From Friday night to Sunday morning, don't look at the computer or take phone calls or even study material from your office. Give yourself the equivalent of a Sabbath, and you will return to work more refreshed than ever.

▪ *Watch your diet.* Your brain needs the right foods to work at optimal strength. Eliminate the three white poisons: sugar, salt, and flour. Avoid bread, desserts, soft drinks, and pasta. Instead eat fruits, vegetables, and high-quality proteins such as fish, eggs, or lean meat.

▪ *Get lots of exercise.* The benefits of exercise are chemical. When you exercise vigorously, your brain releases endorphin—the "happy drug"—that makes you feel more positive, confident, and creative.

▪ *Start your day right.* Start by exercising thirty to sixty minutes after you wake up, then eat a high-quality, high-protein breakfast. You will be set up for the day, ready to perform at your best.

Choose Quiet and Solitude

Our lives are filled with sounds that block off communication and interaction. Keep the television and, especially in the car, the radio off. Take advantage of the quiet time to talk to your family or to read or listen to educational, motivational, or inspirational materials. With DVR service, it's possible today to choose to sit in front of the television later, at certain convenient times. The TV or radio should not be used to fill up a void.

Daily periods of solitude are also important. Take thirty to sixty minutes a day to sit in silence with yourself. You will be surprised at the insights and ideas that emerge in the silence. You will also get a chance not only to plan your day, but to clearly think about what you want in the short and long term. Practicing solitude on a regular schedule will give the calm, creativity, and relaxation required for great leadership. French writer Blaise Pascal wrote, "All the problems in the world originate because of man's inability to be alone in a room with himself."

Maintain a Balance Between Life and Work

Workaholics are not effective. And often, people who bring work home do so because they don't have disciplined habits in the workplace. They waste time during the day socializing and then find that they have to work in the evening or on weekends. It is important to maintain a balance between your work life and your personal life. When you go home, resolve to set the business aside and spend quality time with your family.

Control Is the Key to Happiness

According to the Law of Control, happiness depends on how much you feel you are in control of your life.

Unhappiness is the degree to which you feel that you are not in control, or that your life is controlled by outside factors or by other people.

Psychologists refer to our "locus of control." You have an internal locus of control when you are in charge, when you determine what happens to you. It makes you feel strong and purposeful. You have an external locus of control when you feel that you do not control your life. Circumstances, other people, but even your own personality traits can be allowed to control what happens to you. For example, some people know that they have bad tempers that undermine their effectiveness in working with others. But they absolve themselves of responsibility by saying, "Well, that's just the way I am."

Leadership is about responsibility, and that includes the responsibility for taking control of your life and ensuring your happiness.

TWENTY-ONE

Integrity: The Essential Quality of Leadership

IN AN EXECUTIVE boardroom, I once heard one of the richest men in America make a statement that I never forgot. "It seems to me," he said, "that integrity isn't really a value in itself; it is simply the value that guarantees all the other values."

Whenever I hold a strategic planning session, the first value that all the executives agree on is integrity. Leaders know that integrity, trust, and credibility are the foundations of leadership. Leaders stand up for what they believe in.

Winners Never Cheat

Jon Huntsman, Sr., is a multibillionaire who started a chemical company from scratch and grew it into a $12 billion enterprise. His book, *Winners Never Cheat*, is filled with stories taken from his own experience in which he steadfastly refused to compromise his principles. Huntsman says that integrity is the reason that he has been as successful as he is. "There are no moral shortcuts in the game of business—or life," he writes. "There are, basically, three kinds of people: the unsuccessful, the temporarily successful, and those who become and remain successful. The difference is character."

There are many examples of temporary winners who won by cheating. For a number of years, Enron was cited as one of America's most innovating and daring companies. The CEO of the company knew the most important people in the country, including the president of the United States. Except that Enron's success was built on lies, and the "winners" who headed the company are case studies in lack of integrity. You may have heard of Kenneth Lay and Jeffrey Skilling, the fallen CEO and COO, respectively, of Enron. They dominated the headlines for many months, while Jon Huntsman, Sr. (the father of the 2012 presidential candidate), continues to run his billion-dollar company far from the limelight. Leaders with integrity may not be the most famous or flashy of leaders, and they don't care. Integrity means doing the right thing because it is the right thing to do. And that's what makes success.

Leaders keep their promises. They give promises carefully, even reluctantly, but once they have given that promise, they follow through on that promise without fail. And they always tell the truth. Jack Welch calls it "candor." He believes that if you are afraid of candor, then you don't have the guts to be an effective leader. You are going to surround yourself with yes people who will say what you want to hear instead of saying the truth. A leader with integrity is not afraid to face the truth. Welch calls this the reality principle, or "seeing the world as it really is, not as you wish it to be." It is perhaps the most important principle of leadership and dependent on integrity because it demands truthfulness and honesty. Many companies and organizations fail because they don't follow the reality principle.

Integrity means telling the truth even if the truth is ugly. Better to be honest than to delude others, because then you are probably deluding yourself, too.

Leaders need to be confident, but they also need to be open to the idea that they could be wrong. There are many leaders who eventually fail because they refuse to question their own assumptions or conclusions. Alec Mackenzie once wrote, "Errant assumptions lie at the root of every failure."

There's a difference between being confident and blind. Let's face it, in today's world of rapid change, there is a possibility that you are partially wrong or even completely wrong. Maybe you are not wrong, but just opening yourself to that possibility is going to make you a more effective leader because it will open your mind to new ideas or new thinking.

No Exceptions

As a young man, Abraham Lincoln worked as a clerk at a general store. One day, he realized a customer had overpaid by a few pennies. Lincoln set out to find her, walking several miles to return the pennies to the customer. The story got around and soon Lincoln earned the nickname "Honest Abe." Later, his unimpeachable honesty and integrity were key factors in helping President Lincoln lead the United States through the most traumatic period in its history, when the very survival of the nation was at stake. With the exception of George Washington, Lincoln is the most admired and respected president of the United States for what he was able to accomplish, but at the heart of his accomplishments was the same integrity that pushed a young Lincoln to return a few pennies to that customer.

There should be no exceptions to honesty and fairness. For Abraham Lincoln, the fact that the customer overpaid by just a few pennies made no difference—the fact is that she was owed money and it didn't matter how much. If you are willing to compromise on the small situations, the ones that "don't matter that much," then it becomes very easy to compromise on the big circumstances. Integrity is a state of mind and is not situational.

Leaders always err on the side of fairness, especially when other people are unfair. As a matter of fact, the true mark of leadership is how fair you can be when other people are treating you unfairly.

Seven Steps to Leadership

Let's finish by looking at seven steps or tenets to becoming a leader:

1. *Desire.* You must genuinely want the experience and the responsibility of leadership.

2. *Decision.* Make a decision that you are going to pay the price and practice these tenets of leadership.

3. *Determination.* All leaders have great determination in the formative parts of their careers, both to become leaders and to stay leaders.

4. *Discipline.* Self-discipline is key. Your ability to gain self-mastery and self-control will be the critical determinant of how high you rise to the top levels of leadership.

5. *Role modeling.* Learn from leaders that you admire; think about how you can incorporate their behaviors into your behaviors.

6. *Study.* Read books on leadership, take courses on leadership, and learn what effective leadership is. Always think about how you can apply what you are studying.

7. *Practice, practice, practice.* Leadership can be learned. Leadership must be learned. Leadership is the greatest and most pressing need of our civilization. Today as never before, you are needed in the ranks of leadership.

If you practice the ideas and techniques that this book has talked about and you repeat them over and over again, then you will create a clear mental picture of yourself as a leader and you will inevitably become the leader that you dream of being.

INDEX

ABOUT THE AUTHOR

Brian Tracy is a professional speaker, trainer, seminar leader, and consultant, and chairman of Brian Tracy International, a training and consulting company based in Solana Beach, California.

Brian bootstrapped his way to success. In 1981, in talks and seminars around the U.S., he began teaching the principles he forged in sales and business. Today, his books and audio and video programs—more than 500 of them—are available in 38 languages and are used in 55 countries.

He is the bestselling author of more than fifty books, including *Full Engagement* and *Reinvention*.